The Secret under the Tree

CREATED BY

Gertrude Chandler Warner

ILLUSTRATED BY

Kay Life

Albert Whitman & Company

Morton Grove, Illinois

You will also want to read:

Meet the Boxcar Children

A Present for Grandfather

Benny's New Friend

The Magic Show Mystery

Benny Goes into Business

Watch Runs Away

Benny's Saturday Surprise

Library of Congress Cataloging-in-Publication Data

Warner, Gertrude Chandler, 1890-1979
The secret under the tree / created by Gertrude Chandler Warner ;
illustrated by Kay Life.
p. cm. — (The adventures of Benny and Watch ; #7)
Summary: When Benny decides to dig a hole in the backyard,
Grandfather gives him an old map that leads to a special discovery.
ISBN 978-0-8075-0643-1 (pbk.)
[1. Buried treasure — Fiction. 2. Time capsules — Fiction.
3.Grandfathers — Fiction.] I. Life, Kay, ill. II. Title.
PZ7.W244 Se 2001   [E] — dc21   00-010256

Henry

Jessie

Violet

Grandfather

Watch

Benny

The Boxcar Children

Henry, Jessie, Violet, and Benny Alden are orphans. They are supposed to live with their grandfather, but they have heard that he is mean.

So the children run away and live in an old red boxcar. They find a dog, and Benny names him Watch.

When Grandfather finds them, the children see that he is not mean at all. They happily go to live with him. And, as a surprise, Grandfather brings the boxcar along!

Benny Alden loved to dig. In the
winter, he dug snow out of the
driveway.

In the summer, he helped
Grandfather dig his garden.
Sometimes he dug just for fun.
He liked to see what he could
find.

Watch liked to dig, too.

He dug holes to find things.
He dug holes to bury bones.
Sometimes he dug just for fun.

One day when Benny got up, he felt like digging. "Can Watch and I dig a hole in the backyard?" Benny asked Grandfather at breakfast.

"I guess so," Grandfather said.

"Where should I dig?" said Benny.

Grandfather thought for a minute. Then he went into his big closet. He looked in one box. Then he looked in another box.

"Here it is!" he said at last, holding up a very old piece of paper.

"What's that?" asked Benny.
"It's a map," said Grandfather.
"It will show you a good place to dig."

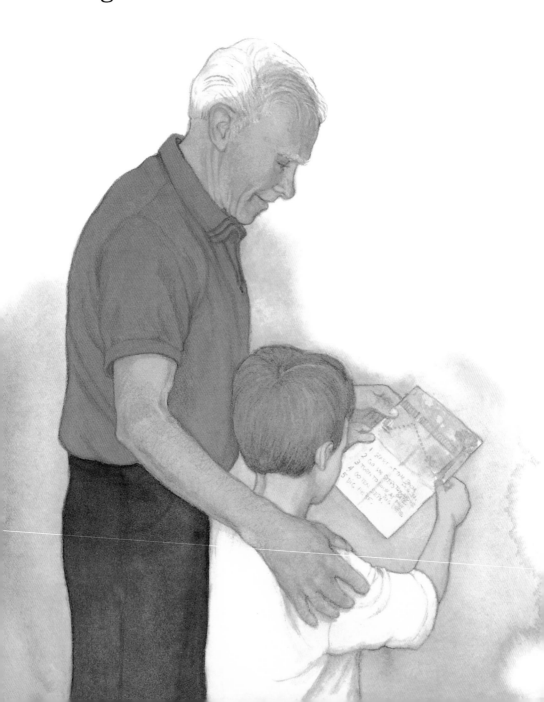

Benny looked at the map. It said:
1. Start at the back porch.
2. Go six steps toward the gate.
3. Turn to look at the big tree.
4. Go ten steps.
5. Dig here.

1. START AT THE BACK PORCH.
2. GO SIX STEPS TOWARD THE GATE.
3. TURN TO LOOK AT THE BIG TREE.
4. GO TEN STEPS,
5. DIG HERE.

Benny got his shovel. He started at the back porch. He walked six steps toward the gate. He turned to look at the big tree. He walked ten steps.

"This is it!" he said to Watch.
"Let's dig!"

"What are you looking for?"
asked Henry, Benny's brother.
"I'm not sure," said Benny. "I'll
know when I find it."
Watch found part of an old
tire.
Benny didn't find anything.
He worked all morning.

After lunch, Benny began again.
"Aren't you getting tired?" asked Violet, Benny's sister.
"Nope," said Benny. "I'm very strong."

The hole was getting bigger. The digging was getting harder.

"Are you going to give up?" asked Jessie, Benny's other sister.

"I don't give up," said Benny.

Watch gave up. He took a nap.
But all afternoon, Benny kept
working. He stopped only once, to
eat an ice cream cone.

Then he started to dig again.
Suddenly his shovel hit
something hard. Benny scooped
the dirt away with his hands. It
was a box! An old, old wooden
box!

Benny tugged and pulled until
the box came out of the dirt. Then
he ran inside to show Grandfather.

Grandfather took the top off the box. Inside was another box! It was made of metal.

Benny opened the metal box.
Inside that was a glass jar!
Benny looked into the jar. There was a piece of paper, all rolled up, and an old photograph.

Benny unrolled the paper very carefully. There was a message on it. The message said:

I AM WRITING THIS ON MY BIRTHDAY.
I AM EIGHT YEARS OLD TODAY.
MY DOG'S NAME IS MAX.
IF YOU FIND THIS BOX, WRITE ANOTHER MESSAGE.
THEN PUT THE BOX BACK IN THE GROUND.
    —FROM JAMES HENRY ALDEN

Benny looked at the photo. There, under the big tree, was a boy with a shovel. Next to him was a dog.

"Wow!" said Benny. "I *did* find something good. James Henry Alden—that's you, Grandfather!"

Grandfather laughed. "It *is* me," he said. "When I was a boy, I loved to dig, too. I buried this box on my eighth birthday. My mother took the picture of me and Max. He was a great dog."

"Maybe that's why *I* like to dig," Benny said. "Because I'm your grandson."

"Maybe so," Grandfather said, giving Benny a hug.

Benny got a piece of paper
and a pencil. He wrote:

I AM SEVEN YEARS OLD. MY DOG'S
NAME IS WATCH.
IF YOU FIND THIS BOX, WRITE
ANOTHER MESSAGE.
THEN PUT THE BOX BACK IN THE
GROUND SO ANOTHER PERSON CAN
FIND IT.
—FROM BENNY ALDEN

Violet took Benny's picture.

When it was ready, Benny put the picture and the message into the glass jar.

He put the glass jar into the metal box.

He put the metal box back into the wooden box.

Benny set the box back into the
ground.
Watch helped put the dirt back.

Benny made a new map. He put
the map in a box in his closet.

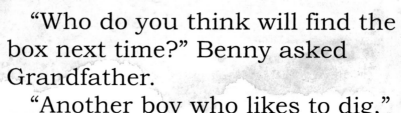

"Who do you think will find the box next time?" Benny asked Grandfather.

"Another boy who likes to dig," said Grandfather. "Just like you and me."